To live an *extraordinary life* is to pursue your purpose boldly, fulfil your dreams courageously, and touch the world with your presence.

Featured Writers

Meet our featured writers for *Extraordinary Life Magazine!*

Emily Gowor

Inspirational Writer, Author & Keynote Speaker

Founder of *Extraordinary Life*

Rieta Mistry

Feng Shui, Numerology, Colour & Flow Consultant

Dr Olivier Becherel

Personal Leadership Specialist, Life & Business Strategist

Michael Bromley

Martial Artist, Teacher & Mentor

Chanthy Ly

Holistic Wellness Coach, Therapist, Chef & Author

Mama Rae

Soul Food Cook & Universal Mum

Editorial

Dear readers,

In every moment of our journey, we are faced with two choices. One, to give up and let go of what we truly want. Or two, to decide that we will do whatever it takes to fulfil our purpose. The decisions that we make day-by-day – and especially in moments when we feel the most challenged – are what ultimately define our life and, therefore, our destiny.

In this issue, our writers will inspire you to take the road less travelled and consciously create the life you truly deserve: the one that lights you up from within and brings out the best of you.

From setting your goals and intentions for the future to the power of rituals and renewing your commitment to your business, you will be supported and encouraged to rise up into who you are and *thrive* on your path of purpose.

I know that creating a life full of meaning and accomplishment isn't always easy. I know that you are likely to experience self-doubts, setbacks and falls along the way. However, don't give up, because *great things* await you in the future.

Welcome to issue 2 of *Extraordinary Life!*

With inspiration,

Inspirational Writer, Author & Keynote Speaker
Founder of *Extraordinary Life*

Contents

Issue 02

INSPIRATION & SPIRITUALITY

ACHIEVEMENT & STRATEGY

WELLNESS & NOURISHMENT

RESOURCES

Article Inquiries

Would you love to write for *Extraordinary Life Magazine*?

Do you have wisdom and inspiration that can make a difference in people's lives?

Would you love to share your personal story of overcoming adversity?

Apply to be a writer!

www.extraordinarylifemagazine.com

Inspiration
&
Spirituality

Create the Extraordinary Life You Deserve

Inspirational writer Emily Gowor shares the first 3 steps to design and manifest an inspiring future

In 2007, at just 19 years old, I experienced a rock-bottom moment where I considered ending my life. I had dropped out of university the year before. I had no job, $2.16 to my name, and no plans.

I faced a deep depression where I was struggling with my self-worth and unsure what to do with my future. I had fallen between the cracks between school and life.

As I laid on the living room floor of my apartment one night, I remember thinking to myself, 'I don't care if my heart ever beats again.' I felt lost, hopeless and vulnerable. But in my moment of greatest struggle when I was questioning whether there was any value to my life, I encountered a destiny-defining epiphany.

Underneath my pain, I didn't believe that we are put here on Earth to suffer. I didn't believe I was put here for an average existence. Instead, I believed the *true* purpose of life is to live fully and wholly, expressing who we are and living an authentic life.

I believed in the spiritual magnificence of life and that every human is being guided to follow and fulfil their higher destiny in each moment and every day.

And so, I made a decision from deep within **to do whatever it took to live an extraordinary life.** As it turned out, that decision proved to be everything I needed to turn my life around.

Within a year, I had rediscovered my love of writing and self-help, and started my business as a professional writer. I was off and running, living a life on purpose – and the rest is history.

Today, I truly believe in my heart that you deserve to thrive. I believe that your life on Earth is anything but random and that you are meant to be here. I believe the greatest gift you can give to yourself and the world is to make your time here extraordinary: to create a life that is filled with achievements, moments, people, relationships, wellness and the wealth you dream of.

But where do we start in creating that extraordinary life for ourselves? It can seem like a gargantuan and overwhelming task.

Here are the first three steps I recommend if you are at a crossroads, a breakdown moment, or simply *ready* to transform your life and fulfil your potential.

1: Your Purpose

Your purpose relates to **who you are** and **what you love to do.** It is by far the most important starting point for a fulfilling life. Why? Because without that central connection to a higher sense of destiny, your life will feel empty, random or meaningless. Discovering your purpose requires knowing yourself deeply: how you are wired, what interests you, and what inspires you. Ask yourself these questions:

- **What do I love to do?**
- **What is my greatest gift?**
- **What do I feel I was born to do?**

Answer openly, intuitively, and honestly. You might even add these questions to your journal and carry them with you over the coming days, weeks, or months. As you answer them, your purpose will become clear.

Although it may seem elusive at times, your purpose is within you. The truth is there, in your heart, and it is the key that you need to move forward. It is the starting point for your life and the essential building block that you can create your extraordinary future from.

2: Your Dream Life

Once you are clear on your purpose, you can start to design the life you dream of for yourself using your purpose as the centerpiece, the guide, and the inspiration.

- **What do you want your days to be filled with?**
- **What does your dream career look like?**
- **Who do you want to spend your time with?**
- **What experiences would you love to have?**
- **What would you love to devote your life to?**
- **What are the most important things your life must have in it for you to feel fulfilled?**

As you sit there reading this, you might have doubts about whether it is possible – or not possible for *you* – to experience this life. If that is true, then I want to encourage you to *open your heart to life*. Allow yourself to dream, truly dream, for yourself and your future.

3: Your Goals

With your purpose clear and your dream-life vision in mind, you can set the goals for your life. The goals will help you to focus each day and get into action creating what you would love.

They will give you the inspiration to move forward and fulfil your purpose on Earth. I typically set the following goals for myself:

- **Lifetime goals**

  Example: Help 10,000 families to embrace holistic parenting approaches.

- **10 year goals**

  Example: Achieve financial independence.

- **3 year goals**

  Example: Grow my business to $500,000 a year annually.

- **1 year goals**

  Example: Write and publish my first book.

- **3 month goals**

  Example: Build and launch my personal brand as a speaker, writer and coach.

Make sure your goals align with your soul's purpose and your dream life. Ask: *Does achieving this support me to fulfil my purpose?* This will help you to use your time wisely and manifest powerfully.

I'm a big believer that simple works best when it comes to goal setting. Be clear on what you would specifically like to achieve, but don't overthink it too much.

A reminder: it's better to have fewer goals and have them *inspire* you than to write 50 goals that don't ignite you from within.

Creating the future you dream of may not happen overnight, and it may not always be easy. In fact, it may be the greatest personal growth path you take, as achieving your dreams will invite you to expand your idea of who you are every single day.

But it is worth every effort, because this is your *life* and you deserve to experience the very best version of it.

A deep and undying commitment to give yourself an extraordinary life will be your greatest inspiration on the journey.

You will be pushed and tested as you move forward on your path, and it is your commitment – to your purpose, to your dream, to what you know innately is possible for your life – that will encourage you endlessly.

In each moment, that commitment to fulfil all you are capable of will call out to you and move you infinitely. That is why you need it so much because it is in remembering that you are here for a reason (and that reason is meaningful) that you won't give up.

So, piece by piece, beginning right from where you are today, start to establish a new life for yourself. Create a life that has deep meaning, that inspires you to tears, that fulfils you in ways you never dared dream possible. A life that is original and unique to you.

A life that is filled with everything that has meaning for you. A life that inspires the deepest levels of your being. A life that brings you to life. That is what you are here for. Settle for nothing less.

Emily Gowor is an Inspirational Writer, Author & Keynote Speaker devoted to helping people fulfil their purpose on Earth.

www.emilygowor.com

Become the Visionary Artist of Your Life

How to honour your soul's calling and activate your creative power

When you think of an 'artist', what comes to mind? Do you think of a painter? A musician? A sculptor? A filmmaker? Did you know that regardless of whether you believe you have a creative bone in your body, you are in fact an artist? Yes, you.

Let's take a look at the official definition. According to the Merriam Webster Dictionary, an artist is 'a person who creates art using conscious skill and creative imagination'. Now let's examine the definition of 'art'. One definition says art is 'the conscious use of skill and creative imagination, especially in the production of aesthetic objects'.

What aesthetic creation could be more worthy of skill and creative imagination than that of a life we are truly moved, touched and inspired by? One that sees us deeply connected to the magic and beauty that surrounds us. One that has us fully immersed in the divinity that exists within.

Creating this kind of life, one that truly feels like an exquisite masterpiece, requires you to activate the visionary artist within. This is the part of ourselves that carries a spark of the divine, continuously orienting us to our highest purpose, our creative power, and our deepest truth. It calls us to create the art we are meant to actualise in our lifetime in accordance with our soul's deepest desires.

The visionary artist is equal parts visionary and artist. A perfect balance between yin and yang. Masculine and feminine energy. Energies of polarity working together in perfect harmony. The **visionary** is able to tap into this universal flow from which all things are possible. They see far beyond what is present in our current reality. They see potential and possibility. They are in constant commune with the divine. The visionary says to the artist, "I see potential here. We are being called here. Let's pursue this. Let's create this." The visionary plants the seeds, while the **artist** brings those seeds to fruition through their creations. They are the one who makes the unmanifest, manifest. Together they are the visionary artist.

Of course, this sounds wonderful in theory, but we all know how easily life can become challenging and overwhelming. It is so easy to find ourselves disconnected from our soul's essence, disconnected from the immense creative power our visionary artist wields. So, when you find yourself stuck in the vicissitudes of life, how do you activate the visionary artist within so you can truly live the life your soul is deeply calling you to create?

First, we must invite the visionary to dream and allow the artist full permission to create their art. If we do not believe we are deserving of the dreams that have been gifted to us – if we do not believe we are worthy vessels for the universe to express and create through us – our visionary artist loses its source of creative power.

Second, we must distinguish between the voice of the visionary artist that emanates from our soul and the voice of the ego self. For the majority of humanity, the ego self is the dominant voice that controls and rules our lives. As visionary artists, we commit to choosing the voice of our soul in each moment. This is difficult at first. The ego voice will try to infiltrate our thoughts, our feelings and our creations at every turn.

Sometimes we may even think we are acting from the visionary artist's guidance when, in fact, it is the ego self in disguise. The more we practice this distinction, the easier it becomes. The vision our soul has for ourselves and our lives becomes a self-fulfilling prophecy – an inevitable reality.

Third, we must trust in the universe's timing and surrender to the visionary artist's lofty ideals. The choices the visionary artist will be guided to make won't always make logical sense. The challenge for our human side is to trust this process and surrender resistance. Can we allow our visionary artist to create in accordance with the universe's timeline without our ego mind interfering? Can we trust the unfolding?

When you truly commit to activating the visionary artist within, you will experience a creative fire far beyond what you previously thought possible. You will become witness to a life that is rich with beauty, purpose and meaning. It won't always be smooth sailing, but once the fire is lit, there will be no stopping it. All that will be left to do is sit back and watch your masterpiece unfold.

Hannah Rose Deacon is a multidimensional artist, songstress, and life and business mentor helping entrepreneurs activate their inner visionary artist and tap into the magic and flow of life.

https://brandalchemyacademy.com/

"Let nothing stop you and stop at nothing on the journey of living your dreams."

EMILY GOWOR

Grounding Practices to Start Your Day

Suzanne Kennedy shares 8 simple practices to help you energise and align yourself each morning

Grounding is very important for our wellbeing in life. We are all made up of energy within our physical bodies. We can pick up lots of varying negative energy from the toxins in the air, from the food we eat, and from the people we are around. We can also experience negative energy internally, through our emotions and thoughts.

All of this can 'dull our sparkle'. We may feel very off balance, tired, or unable to cope with everyday life. We are here on Mother Earth to shine our brightest light, and so, luckily, there is a way we can fix this.

Grounding our energies can be such a simple thing to do for our wellbeing and to start the day at our highest potential. We can ground ourselves and create our day just as we awaken.

1: Good Morning New Day

Wake up gently. Allow yourself to shift from sleep to waking without rushing or pushing yourself. Next, put both of your feet on the floor while still sitting on the bed. Sit still for a moment. Take time to just breathe.

2: Crystal Vibrations

Choose a crystal that you feel drawn to. Hold it in your hand or place it on your

heart chakra (in the centre of your chest). I also have a rock that has 'thank you' painted on it that I sometimes use for this.

3: Express Your Gratitude

Say, "Thank you for my eyesight, my taste, my touch, my smell, my hearing. Thank you for the happy and healthy cells within my body. Thank you for giving me the opportunity to sleep next to my husband. Thank you for this new day. How does it get any better than this?"

4: Move Your Body

Rotate your ankles slowly in both directions, shake your shoulders, and rotate your head slowly from side to side and up and down. Make sure to slowly breathe in and out while doing these wakeup exercises, still sitting down on the edge of your bed.

5: Drink Water

A glass of water is always good to drink when you get up to awaken your organs and allow your chi – your life force energy – to flow.

6: Essential Oils

I also use essential oils to benefit my wellbeing when I start my day. Breathing in peppermint oil from the palm of my hand to wake me up, clears the airways and refreshes my senses. I place essential oils onto my pulse points: my wrists, chest, the back of my neck, and the soles of my feet.

Wild orange, lime, bergamot, rosemary, and peppermint are also great uplifting oils. Pure essential oils are scientifically proven to work on the brain and to help empower the mind. Note: Please only use 100% pure essential oils on your skin. They can be mixed with a good carrier oil to help increase the benefits.

7: Walk On The Earth

I then go outside and walk on Mother Earth barefoot. You may wish to wipe your feet on the grass, soil or whatever surface you are on. This is especially amazing when it has just rained! (I advise my clients to do this every morning.) This action grounds you, awakens all your senses and connects you to positive ions in the earth through your feet. It also massages the organ points (reflexology points) on your feet and can be of great benefit to your wellbeing.

8: Breathe Deeply

While you are standing on the grass or other surface, you may wish to spread your arms wide, taking three slow, deep breaths. One breath is for your mind, one is for your body, and one is for your soul. Feel yourself breathe as you are doing this, taking time on each breath. Allow the breath to expand right down to your stomach, to your sacral chakra. Feel yourself and your body healing and letting go.

Take the time to look up at the sky and around yourself to feel how good it is to be alive. Do you feel more centred now? More awake? You are ready to start your amazing day, grounded within. With love and light within you and all around you, thank you, universe, for this special day!

Suzanne Fox-Kennedy is a Reiki Healer & Master who helps people to heal from within and create a life of health and abundance.

@Reiki Healing with Suzanne

Setting Intentions for Your Life

Sani Yamin shares why intentions are the compass we need to navigate to a purposeful and fulfilling life

"You're usually so supportive and know what to say, but not today..." she said, crying. The tearful look on the face of my close friend cut through my heart like a hot knife through butter. She had only just begun to date again after clearing some emotional blockages through therapy, and her new boyfriend had just broken up with her. Without even asking the context of their break-up, I launched into 'Break-up 101', projecting my own experiences onto her situation.

I realised that I'd failed to give her the support that she needed, all because I neglected to set an intention for the way I would show up for her. As someone who prides themselves on being supportive to my friends, it was disheartening that I had dropped the ball on that occasion, but the powerful lesson of setting intentions was learnt that night.

Intention is the muscle around the skeleton of our wellbeing. It coordinates our desires and emotions into purposeful action. It's easy to feel like life is like a raging river dragging you from situation to situation. We move so quickly from one thing to the next that the meaning and intention of our activities often get washed away in our day-to-day busyness.

We've all experienced work meetings where hours of discussion led nowhere or a date night that felt decidedly unromantic because you were both occupied with your phones. If an intention such as 'a decision needs to be made about XYZ in the next 30 minutes' or 'I'm going to turn my phone off tonight so I can be fully present with my partner' was set, then the probability of the desired outcome greatly increases. Setting intentions is about priming your mindset to hold your desired outcome as your north star in any given situation or scenario.

Through the power of our mind's executive centre, the prefrontal cortex, the mind has a stunning ability to focus should we choose to train it through mindfulness and meditation. Setting intentions is another potent way to sharpen the blade of focus and evaporate unwanted outcomes from our decisions.

The beauty of setting intentions is that you can have different intentions across different areas of your life, including your physical and mental health, career, relationships, and finance. It is important to add detail to your intentions and to expand them into measurable goals where the outcome is crystal clear.

For example, instead of simply stating 'I want to be healthy', define what 'healthy' means to you. Does it mean you wake up in the morning with a spring in your step instead of sluggishly sleeping in? Does it mean you can run five kilometres confidently? Take the time to expand your intentions so there is a clear objective that can not only be measured but distinctly felt within your heart and soul.

To begin to move from a reactive life into one of intentional living requires the constant asking of key questions during transitional moments.

- *What do I want to feel in this situation, and how do I want others to feel?*
- *What is my desired outcome, and how do I want that to unfold?*

As you develop your intention, ensure that it is clear and simple. It needs to be in full alignment with your values and free of any resistance or limiting beliefs. Declare your intention aloud, ensuring it can be spoken in one concise sentence. A sense of clarity and empowerment from stating your intention will give you the confidence to achieve your desired outcome walking into any given situation.

To further develop the habit of being intentional, be accountable for the results yielded. Intentions need to be recalibrated and reworded as you move through different situations and life experiences, a never-ending process that leads to profound self-growth.

Similar to a pilot who uses coordinates to plot a course through the skies, our intentions are our subconscious waypoints that chart our growth to our desired destination. Intentional living expands our focus and empowers us to be the truly conscious creators shaping our own destiny one precious moment at a time.

Sani Yamin is a writer, musician and adventurer fascinated by growth, travel, the ocean, music and the mysteries embedded in the soul.

https://saniyamin.medium.com/

The Power of Your Environment

Flow Consultant Rieta Mistry explains why what you have in your space may be holding you back in your life

Did you know that your environment is subconsciously determining the outcomes in your life? Your environment is made up of your home, office, the furniture and artifacts, computer, your phone, your car. Everything your eyes see, your hands touch, your nose smells, and your ears hear make up your environment.

The information you take in from your environment through your senses are interpreted by your brain, which then influences how you feel and react. Research studies have shown that well-lit rooms, whether with artificial light or natural light, significantly help with mental health issues such as anxiety and depression.

Look around your environment. What message is your brain receiving, and how is your body, mind and soul reacting to it?

Here is an example. Look around you in your home: Are your picture frames hung on the wall in a zig-zag fashion (at different heights)? Are the books in your bookshelf stored haphazardly, with the tops of the books at irregular heights (rather than being stored neatly from highest to lowest)? Is life feeling like a bit of a rollercoaster?

Now, let's consider the environment outside your home. The first non-verbal communication you have with the outside world is through your letterbox. What message is your letterbox conveying to the world? Is it rusty? Is it falling apart? Is it hidden? Is it dirty?

A letterbox is not just a box. It is an important part of your environment, as it is the first energy entrance point to your home. Your letterbox needs to have a solid positive energy about it. It needs to be clean and have a good base (this indicates a solid foundation in life). Check to see if the lock on it is secure and tidy. Your letterbox is a statement point, so have one that is unique and represents you and your values.

Remember, everything around you is a reflection of you and your life values. You can have a decorator come and do your interior styling and design, however, be clear and ensure that your identity is not lost and that the images and colours chosen help you to stay in a happy, healthy state of mind and relay abundant positive messages to your brain.

Now, let's head to the front door. This is known as the 'mouth of Qi'. This is the entry of all energy. Qi is the life force energy. You have the power to determine what energy flow you would like to invite into your home and life.

Keep the pathway leading up to your front door clear of obstacles (e.g., potted plants and ornaments). You want your life to flow freely. Often what happens is that we tend to self-sabotage, and we put obstacles in our own way. We keep physical clutter and obstacles at the front door and then we wonder why life feels so blocked and why there are no opportunities opening up for us. Remember, your eyes are seeing all this clutter, and it sends the message to your brain saying, 'There's no room here for anything new.' When your brain gets that message, your whole body and being vibrates that energy. What your eyes see is very, very, very important.

The first thing to do for your door would be to use some orange spray and give your door a good clean. The reason we use orange spray is because orange is the colour of change. As you are cleaning the door, set a firm and clear intention of the energy you are prepared to allow into this sacred space of yours. Ensure there is some space between your front door and the furniture or artifacts. This represents your career path, so it is important that this is kept clear, allowing you the opportunity for a career change or career improvement to manifest.

The way your environment is set up has the answers to some of the obstacles you are currently facing. We subconsciously place items or use colours in our space that are detrimental to our journey, either because we are afraid of success or afraid of judgment, or because we have a belief that we don't deserve the best.

Your environment plays a major role in your mental and emotional wellbeing. This translates to all areas of your life, be it a relationship, your health, your career or your abundance. You are worth it! You deserve the best! Success is your birthright! Reclaim your power by reclaiming your environment.

Rieta Mistry is a Flow Consultant who uses the power of colour, numerology, and Feng Shui to support people in manifesting the life they dream of.

www.rietamistry.com

Extraordinary Story: The Healing Power of Our Pets

Our pets are natural born healers. How do I know this? I had an amazing dog, Bear, a Jack Russell who recently crossed the rainbow bridge, leaving me heart broken.

When you have a strong connection with your pet, they communicate with you on levels that some people don't understand.

I met Bear when she was nine weeks old. I knew she would change my life, although I didn't realise just how much. I had experienced more trauma than most people do in a lifetime.

It started in year 8 when I was bullied by a group of girls for two years, even though the police and school principal were involved. I was taunted, humiliated, called names and physically pushed around.

At 18, I was raped. In my early 20s I was in a domestic violence relationship where I was hit and pinned against the walls and the floor. This lasted for several months before I had the courage to leave. After this, I went off the rails partying with friends.

During the next few years, I became sick, and after visits to various doctors, antibiotics, a hospital stay and many tests, I had a colonoscopy and was finally diagnosed with Crohn's disease.

At 34, I met someone who later became my fiancé, and we moved to the country. I had two miscarriages. After the second one, I was diagnosed with having a partial molar pregnancy. I was having a blood test every week for six months then fortnightly along with abdomen and chest X-rays. If any tissue had remained, it would possibly turn cancerous. After a year, I finally got the all-clear. However, our relationship didn't survive.

By 2014, I was physically and mentally at rock bottom. I decided to take my life. At the moment where I was about to drop the hairdryer into the bath, all three of my pets – Bear, Angel and Mr Puss – came rushing in and sat on the bathmat staring at me. The look Bear gave me said so much: 'You can't do this! You can't leave us! Who will look after us and love us?'

Since that experience, I have spent the last eight years working on myself, building a stronger, better version of myself. I've been improving my mental and physical health by going to the gym and focusing on positives. Bear helped me in ways medical professionals would not have been able to. She brought me back to life, helped heal my broken heart, and gave me the ability to trust and laugh again. She gave me my life back. Bear not only saved my life, but she provided me with the strength to rebuild my life.

Although the grief I have suffered since losing Bear has been at times unbearable, I have dedicated my life to helping others navigate their own grief of losing a pet by writing a book called *The Bear Project*.

Jody Crossley is a writer, animal lover, and advocate for mental wellness around pet grief.

Quick Takeaways

1

Discovering your purpose, seeing your dream life clearly, and setting your goals are the first three steps to creating an extraordinary life.

2

Grounding your energy first thing in the morning can set you up for wellness and fulfilment each day.

3

Allow your visionary artist to emerge and work with your creative powers as you manifest the life you would love.

Quick Takeaways

4

Your environment has the power to influence your mood, thoughts, feelings and direction in life. Be conscious of what you keep in your physical space.

5

Setting clear intentions for each day and each moment of your life will guide you to experience more of the magic, connection and meaning that is available for you.

6

No matter what you have faced in your life, there is always a way to overcome your adversities, heal, and find a new way forward.

Achievement & Strategy

The Power of Rituals & Habits for High Performance

Learn how to stair-step your way to personal and professional success with the power of consistency

Rhythm is everywhere. Our lives are orchestrated or guided every day by the rising and setting of the sun and the moon, the changes in temperature from day to night and from season to season, the tidal ebb and flow, and by our own internal rhythm.

We also find rhythm in our breath, in our heartbeats, in the language we speak. These are constant reminders of life's pulsing rhythm that moves within and around us.

As much as we wish for each day to be different, the cycle of repeating the same actions day after day is common. That's why habits and rituals are an important part of our lives.

While we often tend to use the words 'habit' and 'ritual' interchangeably, they are very different. The main distinction between habits and rituals is *how aware and intentional we are.*

What is a habit?

A habit is an activity you have repeated so often that it becomes automatic.

A habit usually manifests itself as an *urge* to do something and is often triggered by a particular *cue*. ***There is very little energy or thought that goes into it because it's mostly a means to achieve an outcome.***

In contrast, a ritual is the opposite of a habit.

What is a ritual?

Rituals are predefined sequences of actions characterised by rigidity and repetition.

A ritual requires our full presence and attention and *deliberate practice*. Rituals are viewed as more meaningful practices which have a real sense of purpose. ***With rituals, you are fully engaged with a focus on the experience of the task*** rather than its mere completion.

So, both habits and rituals are regular and repeated actions, but habits happen with little or no conscious thought, whereas rituals require a higher degree of intention and effort.

Habits and rituals have different purposes. ***The purpose of habits is energy conservation and optimisation to free up space and time in our minds*** so we can use our energy for solving more interesting, stimulating and valuable problems. A habit solves a recurring problem in our environment without using too much energy and attention.

The purpose of a ritual is to consciously mobilise and direct time and energy into the experience of a task or activity that is believed will create a desired future outcome. A ritual mobilises energy and attention to fully experience a task or activity.

Key Ingredients to Make Habits and Rituals Stick

There are a few reasons why you may be having trouble changing a habit or staying consistent with your chosen ritual.

One may be that the habit or ritual you're wanting to create is not aligned with your true highest values. This creates a lack of drive and meaning to start or maintain it.

Next, you may have an inappropriate system, meaning an inadequate strategy and execution plan. It's too complicated, too hard, or it will take too much time, effort and energy and disrupt your natural daily flow.

Third, your environment may not be conducive to sustaining the habit or ritual. If you want to make a habit or ritual an important part of your life, make visual cues and reminders a big part of your environment to reinforce your behaviour.

Design Your Environment For Success

Let us consider two equations where f means "*a function of.*"

(1) Results = *f* (Behaviour)

(2) Behaviour = *f* (Person, Environment)

These equations mean that (1) ***the results we get in life comes from our behaviour*** *- the activities we do.* (2) ***Our behaviour depends on who we are*** *- Person -* ***and the nature of our surrounding*** *- Environment.*

Our environment is the invisible hand that shapes our behaviour.

Every habit or ritual is context specific and dependent. That means specific activities happen in a certain place at a certain time. The more we can create an environment where everything has a place and a purpose, the more stable the environment is, and the more habits and rituals can easily form.

Before thinking about creating new habits or rituals, first take an inventory of what you are currently doing and evaluate whether it's working for you or not.

- **What habit(s) are currently working well for you?**
- **What ritual(s) do you currently have in place to become who you would love to be?**

Take a moment to reflect and recognise first that you may already be doing something

valuable that you take for granted. Awareness is the step to any transformation, change and growth: awareness of what you currently do, what you would do, and who you would love to become.

To become who you truly could be and have the life you know you are capable of, the next questions to ask yourself are:

- **What habits and/or rituals could help me move closer to my desired goal?**
- **What habit(s) am I wanting to create to solve a recurring challenge?**
- **What ritual(s) am I wanting to put in place to become who I'd love to be?**

The Power of Stacking

A very effective strategy to create a new habit or ritual is to connect what you want to do (new habit or ritual) with something you already do. This is known as 'habit stacking', and the typical formula is:

After [Current habit], I will [NEW HABIT / RITUAL]

Some examples of this could be:

- When I buy a new item, I will give something away (embrace minimalism).
- After I wake up, I will take five minutes to write down my plan for the day (clarity leads to productivity).
- As I sit on the bed before going to sleep, I will think about one thing I'm grateful for today (reflect on your day, set yourself up for a peaceful sleep).

The Hidden Benefits of Rituals

Rituals have been part of human existence for thousands of years. They have been instrumental in building community, promoting cooperation, and marking transition points in a community member's life. Rituals have evolved as distinct features of human culture.

Rituals go further than helping us to live out our values. They may also make us less anxious. Ritualistic practices can help bring a degree of predictability to an uncertain future by convincing our brains of ***constancy and predictability.***

Scientific studies show that the anxiety-reducing effect of rituals can apply to almost any high-pressure endeavour. Research shows rituals improve performance and confidence, and they can even benefit our physical well-being and immune system.

Finally, keep in mind that habits and rituals are meant to serve you for the long term (not stress you out). Establishing them takes time, because it is something that you do every single day: consistency is everything.

So, be creative, experiment, refine, and find the purpose and benefits to help you stick with the new habits and rituals you'd love to bring into your daily life. And, most importantly, make it work for you!

Dr. Olivier J. Becherel, PhD, is a Personal Leadership Specialist, Life & Business Strategist who helps high-achieving professionals to break through to the next level of their life and career.

www.drolivierbecherel.com

Living Your Legacy

Ali & Ron Beswick share 3 ways to get started on living your legacy now rather than just leaving it

You don't have to wait until you've left this realm to start creating and sharing your legacy. You can choose to live it right here, right now.

When most people think of the word 'legacy', they tend to think of it as a bequest: a gift by will, especially money or personal property left to us when someone dies. However, for us, *living our legacy* rather than just leaving it has become a part of our daily lives.

A definition we prefer is that it's about **the richness of the individual's life, including what that person accomplished and the impact they had on people and places.**

Ultimately, the story of a person's life reflects the individual's legacy.

When a dear friend of ours passed away, a poem was read during the celebration of her life. The poem highlighted for us just how authentically she had *lived her legacy*. That poem is 'The Dash' by Linda Ellis:

'I read of a man who stood to speak at the funeral of a friend. He referred to the dates on the tombstone from the beginning ... to the end.

He noted that first came the date of birth and spoke of the following date with tears, but he said what mattered most of all was the dash between those years.

For that dash represents all the time they spent alive on earth and now only those who loved them know what that little line is worth …'

We realised that our friend had in fact not only left a lasting legacy for many people but was also the epitome of someone that *lived her legacy* day in and day out. She truly lived her 'dash'.

Afterwards, we reflected on the poignancy of this. Living *our* legacy is something we made a conscious decision to do many years ago. We were brainstorming what we could leave behind for our family after we died. During our reflection, we suddenly realised that what we did while we were alive and able to spend time with our family and friends probably mattered a whole lot more than after we were gone.

One key aspect for us is living as balanced a life as possible – body, mind and spirit – and being an example in the first instance to our family. We then hope to inspire others through our words and actions.

Another factor is living your values. What do you stand for? We've all heard the saying 'Stand for something or fall for anything!' At the end of your life, what will be important is that you lived your life according to your values.

As Ali's mum often said, "You come into this world with nothing, and you go out of it with nothing. What you achieve along the way is a bonus." While she worked hard for most of her life, she was kind, caring and generous of heart and spirit. This was reflected at her funeral with the massive crowd and beautiful tributes people paid to her. She truly did live her legacy.

How do you start to create *your* living legacy?

1. Be the best you can be: in body, mind and spirit.
2. You don't have to think big to have a BIG IMPACT. Small gestures can often make a big difference.
3. Live a purposeful life and help others in a multitude of ways.

We started by focusing on being the healthiest we could be so we were then able to inspire others to live their best lives. While we're not perfect and we fall off the wagon every now and then, our daily intent is to live *our* best lives, touch other's lives in the best way possible and inspire others to live *their* legacy, too.

Think of the people who have inspired or excited you, mentored or coached you, or perhaps gave you a helping hand through gifting goods, services or moolah. All of these people were living *their* legacy.

A myriad of experiences, memories and moments make up our lives. Take care of these and hold them gently in your hands. This life is less about what we've earned and more about who we've loved. Less about the life lived and more about who you live that life with – in the broader sense – our soul family. As our friend Emily Gowor says, "*Living your legacy* is about every person you touch along the way."

Ali & Ron Beswick are Midlife Reignition Catalysts who help and inspire people to ReWire, not ReTire.

www.aliandron.com

"Live boldly in pursuit of your purpose.
Do what you were born to do."
EMILY GOWOR

Goal Setting with a Difference

Theresa Lynch shares 2 ways to have fun and be creative with goal setting

People set goals because they want to achieve something in their life. This may be a new career, more money, a new home, a life partner, or better health. When people think about setting a goal, many think about using the S.M.A.R.T method.

Now if this works for you, awesome, stick with it. However, I have found a lot of people get frustrated and have given up on setting goals as this method doesn't work for them.

First, you need to form a clear picture of the vision for your life in order to set your goals. Here is an exercise to help you with this. Take out a piece of paper and a paper. You will write three versions of your vision, each one becoming bigger and more inspiring.

Version 1: Visualise what your life could look like in three years' time. By doing this, you will start to see all the things you have accomplished during this time.

Write them down for yourself. It may include things such as what you are wearing, what you are doing, how you are feeling, where you are living and the people around you.

Version 2: Now it's time to dream a little bigger. Think about your life in three years' time and ask yourself what you would really love to accomplish. Write down all the things you think you can achieve in the time frame. It may be to increase your income, change careers, buy a house, travel, a new car or whatever takes your fancy.

Version 3: Once you have written this version, take a few minutes and think about what you have written. If you were to push yourself a bit further, what might you be able to achieve in the same time frame? This time, I want you to imagine that the sky is the limit and anything is possible.

What does your life look like now? Does it feel more exciting? What would your life look like in three years' time if you had no restrictions at all on what would you do?

Write this version down, no matter how far-fetched it sounds to you. Don't listen to that voice that is saying you can't achieve that, it's impossible. Nothing is impossible when we are dreaming.

Once you have written the three versions, I recommend that you put them away for a couple of days. Then come back and read the third (last) vision. Is there anything that you could do to make it happen?

When I did this, one thing I wanted to do was promote my book as a guest speaker on the Dr Phil show. As I don't have a book written, I can start this journey by learning how to write and publish a book.

You may be asking, that's all well and good, but what do I do now? My simple answer is to write it out in steps. I have a specific process I use to write out my steps to achieve what I want. I take an A4 coloured piece of paper and write down my end goal. I then have five pieces of A5 paper, and I write down the steps that I need to take right now to make it happen. I lay them all on the ground, outside if the weather is cooperating, and walk through the steps. I imagine myself achieving each step along the way.

Sometimes in this part of the process you may need to change the order or even remove something and add a different step. These aren't set in concrete, and you may find an easier way to achieve the goal. Check in regularly to see if the goal is still something you want to do and whether you need to add more steps or change some of them around.

Remember, just because you have set a goal doesn't mean you will achieve it. I can hear you say, "Then why should I bother setting a goal?" I can tell you that goal setting is about the journey, not the destination. Know that it is okay to let that goal go. You haven't failed.

You have learnt things that you may not have learnt by setting and working towards that particular goal. You are not the same person who started on the journey. Take some time to reflect on what you have learnt and, when you are ready, set a new goal.

Setting goals is about discovering and learning what you want and even what you don't want in your life. Have fun and experiment with different ideas. There are ways of achieving what you want in your life and remember to enjoy the journey along the way.

Theresa Lynch is a Transformation Coach who helps people to transform their lives.

www.dragonflydreamcoaching.com.au

The Power of Joyful Commitment

Simple strategies that will empower you to elevate your business growth and attract more joy and fulfilment into your life

Most of us are unaware of the four What is your level of commitment to creating a successful business and a life that brings you joy and abundance? How serious are you about achieving your goals? As John C. Maxwell said, '"Dreams don't work unless you do."

Most of us will admit to being hesitant about committing to doing things that scare us. I know I am. For example, you will never in a million years, persuade me to go bungy jumping or sky diving! Yet, I will commit to making decisions that are right for my business and my life, even if acting on those decisions may feel daunting at times. It takes courage to create a business and a life that is uniquely yours. It can be easy to follow what others are doing instead of listening to your inner voice.

Are you truly committed to doing whatever it takes to create a business that brings you joy? Or have you set goals for your business that never come to fruition? Do you sometimes feel like you're a pilot in a plane and you simply can't get the plane off the ground?

One of the driving factors in creating a successful business is committing to stepping out of your comfort zone every day and taking positive action towards achieving your goals. The decisions and actions that have brought you to this stage in your business will be very different from what you need to do to take your business to the next level. The same principles and mindset apply to creating a life that brings you joy and abundance.

Committing to accelerating your business growth involves taking time to pause and reflect on where you are now and where you want to be so that you can create dreams and goals for the next level of your business.

The easiest way to do this is to **schedule a meeting with yourself every month.** You make your clients and other people a priority, don't you? Well, it is even more important to make yourself a number one priority.

Put aside at least an hour for your meeting and find a quiet place where you won't be interrupted by anyone. Take a pen and paper with you and write honest answers to the questions below. Resist the temptation to make notes on your phone.

You'll be amazed at the unexpected thoughts and realisations that appear when you do this exercise. Let go of any self-judgement, guilt, or shame. This process simply helps you explore where your focus is right now and will reveal anything that may be getting in the way of you moving forward in your business.

Ask yourself the following questions:

- Am I committed to creating a successful business, or do I have (or want this to be) a hobby?
- On a scale of 1 to 10, what is my level of commitment to growing my business? (1 being low, 10 being high.)
- What is stopping me from committing to my business growth?
- What actions do I need to START to honour my commitment to my business?
- What actions do I need to STOP if I am to commit to growing my business?
- Who do I need to ask for help from so that I can be accountable for committing to taking action to move forward?
- What people do I need around me who will inspire, empower, and encourage me as I step into taking courageous action every day?
- What people do I need to spend less time with as I commit to growing my business?
- How will I celebrate my decision to commit to my business growth?

Often, the greater your level of commitment to your goals, the more resistance and fear you will feel. That's perfectly natural. Remember it is part of the process and keep taking action anyway. Take small, courageous, positive steps every day. With every courageous step forward that you take as you commit to growing your business, you'll become more of an expert at making brave decisions and taking committed action to achieve your goals.

As you take this positive action, you also send out an energy of clarity and courage that will attract amazing, positive opportunities, and people, to you. Always remember how magnificent and talented you are (especially when you don't feel like that)!

Jean Adams is Business Mentor who is obsessed with empowering female entrepreneurs and business owners in their 50s, 60s and 70s to gain the clarity and confidence they need to enable them to accelerate their business growth.

https://jeanadams.com.au

3 Tips for Marketing Your Business Authentically

How to stay true to your personal values while marketing your business

When marketing a business, many people think they have to compromise their values to succeed, which isn't the case! On the contrary, if you market your business authentically and stay true to your values, you will be more successful than ever.

Marketing your business authentically. What does that even mean?

To market authentically means to be true to yourself and your values. You are not putting on a persona or 'acting' like someone you're not. You are being genuine, transparent, and authentic, which will attract others who also value those things.

What does inauthentic marketing look like?

Providing examples is the best way to highlight the problem with inauthentic marketing. Many coaches and consultants have been taught to hide their pricing and force prospective buyers to sit through a two-hour webinar or book a discovery call before seeing any prices. If you've ever been forced to do this, you know how frustrating it can be!

Additionally, common tactics like false scarcity and FOMO (fear of missing out) are encouraged to create a sense of urgency and increase sales. How would you feel if these tactics were being used on you? Probably not great.

And yet, so many coaches and consultants continue to do these things because they've been told it's the 'right' way to market their business.

The importance of values alignment in marketing

When you use marketing that is aligned with what you value and how you want everyone who touches your brand to be treated, the result is authentic marketing. You know what feels right, and you go with that instinct.

Some examples of values that could guide your authentic marketing strategy include:

- **Connection over conversions**
- **Truth over hype**
- **Service over selling**

The reality is that there is no 'right' way to market your business. There is only the way that feels good for you and aligns with your values. So, if hiding your pricing doesn't feel good or authentic to you, don't do it! Be transparent about your prices from the beginning, and let people decide whether they want to work with you based on that information.

3 tips for staying true to personal values while marketing your business

1. Be clear about your values

The first step is to be clear about what your values are. If you're not sure what your values are, take some time to sit down and brainstorm a list. Once you have a list of values, making decisions that align with those values will be much easier.

Here are a few good questions to clarify your values:

- How do you like to be marketed and sold to?
- How do you want people to feel after working with you?

2. Design positive buying experiences

How do you want people to feel when they interact with your marketing? You're creating anxiety and urgency if you use pressure tactics such as false scarcity and fake countdowns. Is that the feeling you want your potential customers to have? A good question: How can I create a positive buying experience for my potential customers?

Some ideas:

- Create a WOW experience upfront so that they want to work with you
- Offer transparent pricing
- Provide a money-back guarantee
- Make it easy for people to purchase from you
- Be available to answer questions

3. Show that your solution works

Use social proof such as case studies, testimonials, and customer reviews to show that your solution works. This will help build trust and credibility with potential customers and show that you're not just selling a 'pipe dream'.

By following these tips, you can authentically stay true to your values while marketing your business. As a result, you will attract more of the right clients and customers who value what you do.

Anfernee Chansamooth is a marketing strategist, copywriter, and coach who helps change-makers grow their business and personal brand through authentic marketing.

Quick Takeaways

1

Consistency with small habits and intentional rituals adds up over time. Use your daily rhythms to create the results you desire.

2

You can leave your legacy today by choosing to consciously live your legacy. What you do every day sends a ripple out into the world around you.

3

Setting your goals can be a creative and enjoyable process. Allow yourself to dream bigger, expand what is possible, and step into the limitless.

Quick Takeaways

4

Your personal commitment to your business results sets the bar for what you can achieve. Strengthening your commitment to your career is a key to success.

5

Marketing doesn't have to feel difficult or inauthentic. You can craft a marketing approach for your business that feels right!

6

You have extraordinary power and potential to design and create the career and life that you dream of. Devote yourself to the vision inside your heart.

Wellness & Nourishment

Full Cycle Abdominal Breathing

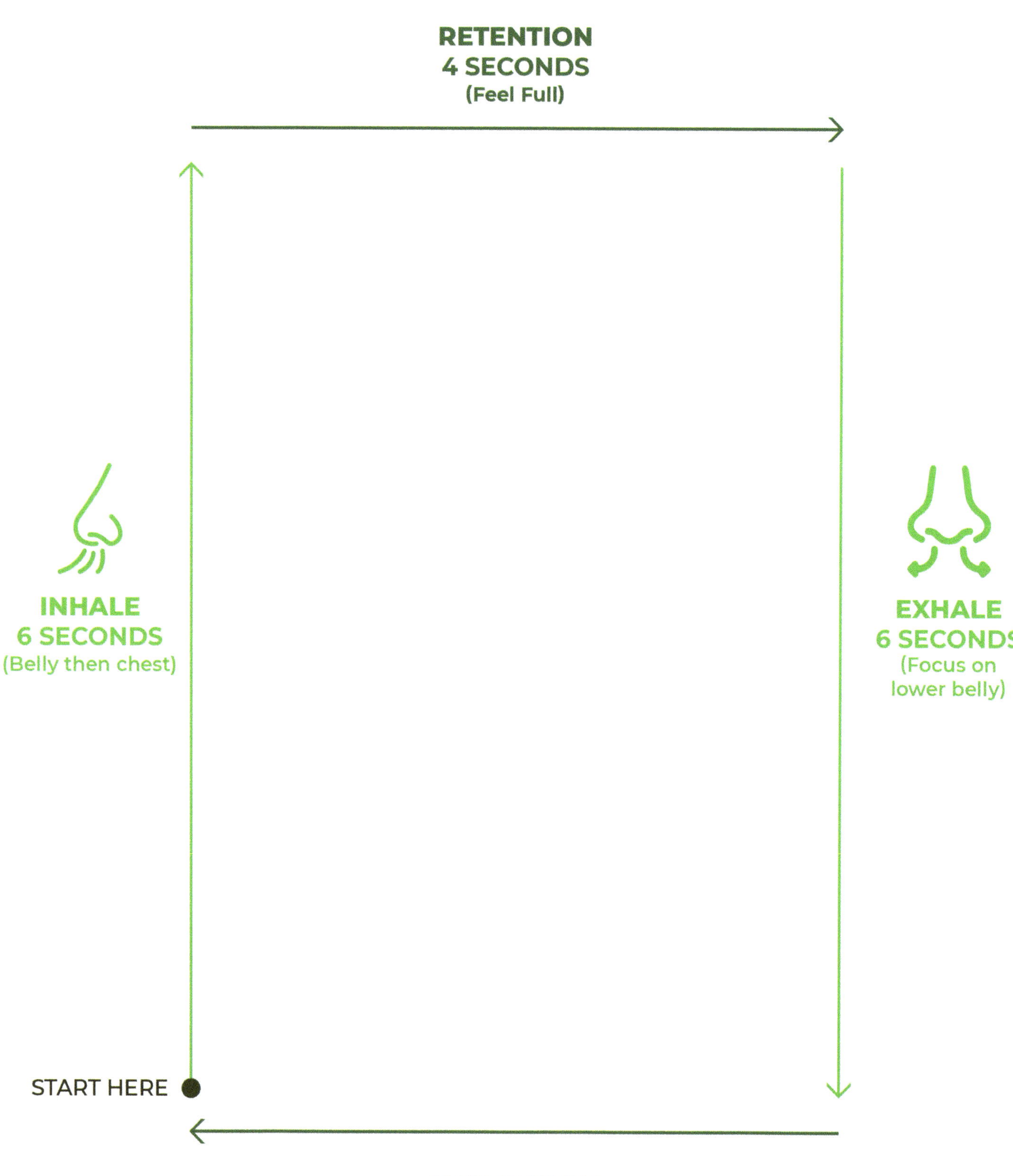

Harnessing the Breath of Life

Discover the transformative power of breathwork and why breathing deeply awakens our potential

Whether we are creating stillness and quiet, increased focus in meditation, or stretching and moving our body, **breathing** is key. It is vital for energy, blood conditioning, oxygenating, detoxing the cells, and aligning with Zen mindfulness.

Deep breathing techniques allow us to consciously and deliberately access Qi (bioelectric) energy and use it effectively. It aids us in co-ordinating spirit, mind, subtle energies and our various bodies.

Although there are many western names for it now, mostly from sport, sport science, neuroscience and the military, we are using the term **'breathwork'** as a general umbrella heading.

What happens when we breathe correctly?

I will talk about nostril breathing in the section below, however, breathing through the mouth is not recommended. There are some techniques that require it, and, of course, we often default to mouth breathing when our heart rate rises during aerobic and anaerobic exercise. However, the absorption rate of oxygen in the body is lessened by breathing through the mouth.

Often, we refer to mouth breathing as shallow or subsistence breathing, and it is generally unhealthy, especially long term and while sleeping. It is best to change our breathing habits to deeper diaphragmatic breathing, belly breathing, and nasal breathing.

This may involve training the diaphragm, just like we would with any other muscle, to become stronger and to 'massage' the stomach and digestive organs, promoting proper elimination (removing toxins from the body).

Through our breath, we have control and our **own power** to restore rest, digestion and relaxation! Here are the foundations of breathwork as we know it today.

Qi Gong – pronounced *chee gong*. This ancient art is a well-known and documented meditative and moving art led by the breath.

Qi Gong has many benefits with immediate effects. Some of these effects include natural detoxing; balancing emotions, stress and focusing the mind in general; improving sleep quality; improving heart health; and the prevention and management of chronic illnesses, diseases, and conditions.

Qi Gong can also support higher levels of fitness (balance, cardiovascular endurance, flexibility, strength and power). It can help with anxiety and mood swings, depression and boost the immune system.

Pranayama – Pranayama is at the core of yoga training. There are many types and methods of this Indian breathwork that span back 4000 years.

It is one of the 8 Limbs of Yoga mentioned in the Vedic texts, including the *Bhagavad Gita* (a Hindu scripture) and the Tattiriya Upanishads in the oral tradition possibly 2500 years ago, but in written form approximately 100 – 50 BCE.

Typically, the Sanskrit meanings translate to:

Prana: Vital life force, breath.

Yama: *simplified*, taking control of suspension, extension, or expansion of breath.

The intention with pranayama is to breathe deeper and actively hold the breath longer. Pranayama practice also means to slow and quiet down the breath, enhancing and nurturing stillness within.

The breath is one of the best-known conscious communications or pathways between the mind and body. Pranamaya, or the vital energy body, regulates and controls the vital functions of our body that are animated by the force of Prana.

The Pancavayu from the Upanishads tells us that Prana governs our inhalation, and the energy moves downward and inward from the head and fills spaces in the cells.

The ancients knew. They mapped out the pathway of energy and vitality in the body and knew that movement should be breath-centric and that our actions are better led with the breath.

What are the benefits of breathing through the nostrils?

Breathing in and out through the nose helps us overcome feelings of stress and promotes a sense of calm. Learning to breathe efficiently is your ticket to greater health and wellbeing on every level. It just takes quality time, some effort and control.

So, make it a positive and joyful experience daily. By the way, this is free!

- Nose breathing helps us take fuller, deeper breaths, which stimulates the lower section of the lungs (in the alveoli) to distribute greater amounts of oxygen throughout the body.

Our sinuses produce a chemical called **nitric oxide** that, when carried into the body through the breath, increases the size of the capillaries and arteries to increase oxygenation.

It also fights harmful bacteria and viruses in our bodies, regulates blood pressure and boosts the immune system.

- Breathing out through the nose slowly helps bleed off carbon dioxide and gives the lungs more time to extract oxygen from the air we've taken in, fill the cells throughout the body, and generally improves your lungs' ability to absorb oxygen.
- Nose breathing maintains proper oxygen to carbon dioxide exchange during respiration, allowing the blood to maintain a balanced pH.
- When we 'mouth breathe', carbon dioxide is lost too quickly. Our oxygen absorption is decreased, which can cause dizziness.
- Nose breathing enables us to slow down until the proper breath is trained.
- Therefore, proper nose breathing reduces hypertension and other cardiovascular problems caused by lifestyle choices, our environment and stress.
- The nose houses *olfactory bulbs* that connect through nerves to the hypothalamus.
- This area of the brain is responsible for many functions in our bodies, particularly those that are automatic, such as blood pressure, the heart's rhythm, thirst, our appetite and sleep cycles.
- The hypothalamus is also responsible for generating chemicals that influence emotion and memory.
- Deep and controlled *Qi Gong and Pranayama breathing* also stimulates the **vagus nerve,** a cranial nerve that starts in the brain stem and extends down below the head to the neck, chest and abdomen, where it contributes to stimulating and communicating with the organs of the body.
- Besides output to the various organs in the body, the vagus nerve conveys sensory information about the state of the body's organs to the central nervous system.

Mouth breathing bypasses the nasal mucosa and makes regular breathing more difficult. Conditions like snoring and sleep apnoea can arise from this. It is typical that people who breathe through the mouth too much are also shallow chest breathers or subsistence breathers.

Essentially, let's avoid the ineffective and unhealthy way of breathing shallowly (especially through the mouth) and instead, focus on breathing more deeply through the nose and into the belly (Hara in Japanese).

Breathe like you are an infant again! The concepts of Qi/Chi/Ki/Prana are intrinsic and reachable resources and partners us to keeping or returning to *nature's way.*

Michael Bromley is a Martial Artist, Teacher, Trainer and Mentor devoted to guiding people on their path of personal evolution.

www.michaelbromley.com.au

Ways To Calm Your Nervous System Naturally

The nervous system is the control centre of the body, sending and receiving signals to and from all parts of the body. There are different divisions of the nervous system.

The central nervous system (CNS) is comprised of the brain and spinal cord. From the spinal cord, the nerves branch out and form the peripheral nervous system (PNS), which processes incoming sensory information.

The autonomic nervous system (ANS), which overlaps partly with the CNS and PNS, has its own nerve chains and regulates involuntary muscles, cardiac muscle, and certain glands. All of this operates outside of our conscious control. There are further divisions within the ANS.

The sympathetic system is responsible for activating our 'fight or flight' or stress response, while the parasympathetic division supports processes that conserve and restore energy during rest and recovery. The body is constantly working to balance these two responses in the nervous system.

Relaxing body treatments like massages and breathwork help stimulate the nerves in the skin, acting on the CNS. This in turn activates the parasympathetic system, sometimes called the 'rest and digest' state. This subdues the stress response, promoting restorative actions, balancing energy and encouraging relaxation.

This state of relaxation helps optimise the functioning of the body systems such as the nervous, circulatory, respiratory and lymphatic system. This allows for the improved oxygenation of tissues, the liver, and other organs, as well as encouraging metabolism and the transportation of waste materials out of the body.

There are Ayurveda-based body treatments that help to pacify the body and strengthen the tissues. They require the application of therapeutic substances such as oils or powders directly onto the body. An example is a classic full body oil massage known as **abhyanga,** which uses warm herbal oil according to the season and the constitution of the person treated.

Oil massages help to moisturise and calm the nervous system, alleviate pain, reduce joint stiffness, boost immunity, and balance hormones. We can also use hot stones and 100% essential oils or a premixed relaxing blend with warm carrier oils such as fractionated coconut oil, sweet almond, jojoba, olive, avocado, or rosehip oil. These all have various healing benefits.

An **herbal bolus massage** uses a muslin bag or bolus filled with herbal preparations heated in oil. The heat aids the absorption of the active ingredients in the herbs. Another treatment known as **shirodhara** involves pouring warm oils or buttermilk in a continuous stream.

It has a powerful effect on the mind, providing deep relaxation, improved concentration and sleep, and easing headaches and depression. It's best done three times in a single session by an experienced therapist to get a full therapeutic regime.

A **steam bath** is a wet heat therapy that aids in the digestion of the oils and herbs applied during a massage, helping to eliminate sweat and pacify nerves. All massages should ideally be followed by a steam bath and performed separately.

A healthy brain and nervous system depend on connections between billions of neurons (nerve cells). Diet, lifestyle, stress, mechanical damage, and ageing can all affect this complex system. Natural remedies and nutrients ease symptoms and support healing.

There are many ways you can improve your parasympathetic nervous system, such as mild exercise or going on grounding walks during the morning or evening. Meditation helps the body decompress and relax. Other activities such as body massages, deep breathwork, asanas, pranayama, yoga, and maintaining a positive energy help reinforce the PNS.

They also improve the ability to maintain your body's balance, rejuvenate the spinal nerves and muscles, alleviate chronic pain, promote healing, improve blood circulation and the lymphatic system, and strengthen your lower back, leg, and arm muscles.

Self-care is also key to great health. Having an evening ritual such as dimming the lights and winding down from blue light exposure, listening to relaxation or sound therapy music, breathwork, or taking a warm bath using essential oils can help start the rest and restoration process before sleeping. All of this is important for repairing your body and rebalancing your nervous system.

Chanthy Thong is a Holistic Health Wellness Coach, Therapist, Chef & Author who is passionate about helping and transforming people health around the world to live and create an extraordinary life.

www.chanthyintowellness.com

4 Pillars of Holistic Parenting

Melissa Hughes shares insights and tools that will ignite a spark of clarity about how you want to raise your children

If you are choosing a holistic approach to raising your children, it's helpful to become clear about what this looks like for your family. There are now many definitions of holistic parenting, with even more misinterpretations, depending who you ask and how the concept is applied.

The good news is that there are four key pillars we can look at that will help form a firm foundation to spring from when it comes to facing the inevitable challenges that come with parenting against the norm.

1. What is holistic parenting to YOU?

According to Google dictionary, the term 'holistic' is '*characterised by the belief that the parts of something are intimately interconnected and explicable only by reference to the whole*'. In this case, we are talking about the various parts that make up the whole of a child, instead of just viewing a child merely as their physical body or developmental milestones.

Things to consider might include their developmental needs as well as their physical, emotional, mental, energetic and spiritual needs or influences. This includes the environment we are raising them within, the impact of the parents and siblings, extended family, friends, peers and the wider community, such as school and television or media.

2. Understand exactly WHY you are choosing this path.

Maybe you feel that you 'missed out' during childhood in some way? You feel that your developmental needs weren't met or perhaps you desired more secure attachments to your parents, knowing now how it impacts aspects of your life. Or maybe your parents were overly authoritarian, and you didn't feel heard.

Showing that you are dedicated to healing and evolving and that you choose differently for your child or children is a beautiful thing. I chose holistic parenting because I know my children are the seeds for the future of humanity. It is an opportunity I choose to partake in wisely, no matter what it takes.

3. What are your values and non-negotiables?

If I asked you right now what your four highest values are, how would you respond? Now look at how often these values are being reflected in your day-to-day life as a family.

Do you have connection as a high value but feel disconnected as a family? Perhaps you could introduce nightly screen-free family dinnertime as an opportunity to connect and debrief. What are your ABSOLUTE non-negotiables? This could be no smacking, naughty corner, forced affection, or punitive discipline. How often do your non-negotiables occur from you or others?

Once we become clear about our non-negotiables, it becomes a lot easier to make better choices and feel more empowered in our parenting.

4. Build your village.

Your support team is made up of members beyond your immediate family who help enable you and your family to thrive. This could be friends, extended family, colleagues, community members and maybe a mentor.

Make no mistake, there will be hurdles and setbacks! This journey is not for the faint of heart. But it is for the courageous and for those with a solid village by their side.

There is a beautiful practice in aware parenting where you have what's called a 'Listening Partner'. This is a support person you can call on a regular basis to share your feelings with that will listen with empathy and without judgement or correction.

Once you map out these four pillars for yourself, you will have a clear pathway to follow when things get dark or if you happen to veer off path. Older children could even be involved in aspects of creating your family map, setting goals and working together to achieve them. It is also important to note that as humans, we will make mistakes. What matters is how we navigate when this occurs, such as apologising for yelling and doing better next time.

It is my deepest wish that these tools support you on your journey, empowering you to become the parent you choose to be.

Melissa Hughes is a Holistic Parenting consultant and founder of the Australian Natural Nanny Network, supporting parents and caregivers to empower kids.

https://naturalnannynetwork.com.au/

Quit the World's Most Popular Drug: Sugar

Deb Peden shares the bitter truth about sweetened foods

I was first alerted to the poisonous nature of sugar when I read David Gillespie's *Sweet Poison*, which linked sugar to soaring obesity levels and to some chronic diseases that have flourished in the twentieth and twenty-first centuries. If you've ever watched episodes of The Simpsons, you'll appreciate the addictive nature of sugar when Homer downs a box of doughnuts, greedily hunting down the sugar treat euphoria.

Paediatric endocrinologist Dr Robert Lustig argues that sugar affects the brain in much the same way as heroin and cocaine. When consuming excessive levels of sugar, there is a change in the gene expression for opioids. Dopamine, the main chemical in the brain's reward system, skyrockets into overdrive every time an addictive substance is consumed, causing us to seek this 'high' repeatedly, a.k.a addiction. In the last 30 years, Type 2 diabetes rates have tripled to 415 million people worldwide. One million of those are Australians! Basically, our food supply has been sweetened (poisoned) by the food industry. Sugar is highly addictive, and it is present in almost 80% of the foods on supermarket shelves: processed foods! Kitchen staples such as breads, tomato sauce, salad dressings, and cereals are often laden with sugar.

There are currently 56 different names ascribed to sugar. Look for these sugar-disguised names when checking out food labels. Here's the full list: https://www.virtahealth.com/blog/names-for-sugar.

As Lustig argues, we've all been 'frucked' by Big Sugar. As a powerful lobbyist for the case against sugar consumption, the battle he faces is akin to the one Jeffrey Wigand faced against the tobacco industry in the 1990s.

The Hollywood film *The Insider* (1999), starring Al Pacino and Russell Crowe, brought the corrupt and life-threatening underbelly of the tobacco industry into sharp and painful focus. However, whereas sectors of the cigarette-smoking public are negatively impacted by tobacco, sugar consumption has an almost blanket consumption rate across the population, often hidden in the many processed foods that fill the supermarket shelves.

Australia is the fifth most obese OECD country: we have 11 million adults and one million children considered overweight! That's two in every three Aussies with an unhealthy body mass index. I believe sugar is the source of much of this problem. Lustig has been arguing for years that sugar is a poison that is wreaking havoc on our health in a range of sinister forms: obesity, heart disease, and cancer! But don't despair: the effects on your health can be reversed very easily if you act before disease sets in. Markedly reducing sugar intake has been shown to have immediate and positive results on overall health.

And if the aging process is of concern, then the sinister news is that sugar accelerates aging. As Lustig tells us, the reason bananas turn brown or the reason we get cataracts or develop wrinkles is because of the Maillard Reaction – a natural aspect of life associated with aging. However, with a largely processed food diet (read sugar and fructose), aging occurs seven times more quickly. This is because we're accumulating seven times the amount of oxygen radicals which cause damage.

The answer, of course, is simple: eat more fibre. In other words, eat *real* food. You know, the items you'd find on the perimeter of the supermarket in the produce aisles. Eat less of what you'd find on the inside aisles where items are labelled. As Lustig would say, 'A food label is a warning label!'

Another key point is that not all calories are created equal (Lustig). Eating 100 calories of sugar and 100 calories of broccoli is not the same. Your body processes those two foods in very different ways; burning off sugar requires much more energy than burning off your greens. Big food companies promote low-calorie food items with the suggestion that they're better for you. Wrong! While sugar is not fat, it converts to fat in your body, especially if your liver is overloaded with sugar.

The brief pleasure that sugar brings is not worth its long-term health-damaging effects.

Deborah Peden supports her clients to balanced health and wellbeing so they can maximise their purpose and potential.

www.100waystoahealthy100.com.au

"No matter where you are today, you can build a deeply meaningful life for yourself."

EMILY GOWOR

The Most Important Ingredient in Cooking: Love

Mama Rae shares why preparing food consciously and with love is nourishing for the mind, body and soul

Although I have been cooking for over 60 years, it is only in the last 20 years that I have understood what it means to eat food that tastes of love. People would compliment me on my cooking, but I didn't really connect what I was feeling and thinking when I was cooking the food to the enjoyment people experienced when eating at my table. After all, I was just cooking... wasn't I?

The fundamental thing I learned was that everything is energy. From the fresh-picked apples to the saucepan they are cooked in, to the words we use or thoughts we have. While they have different densities, they are all energy.

Think about words for a moment. If two people are arguing in the street, you would probably cross to the opposite side to get away from that energy. Whereas, if two people are chatting and laughing, you would most likely want to walk by them. What is the difference? It is that anger and love have different energies, simple as that.

This lesson was first brought to my attention when I had my coffee shop. My daughter, Cassie, would come and make the coffees. I learned that people loved the coffee Cassie made but not mine!

When I examined what we did when we were each making coffee, it was apparent why. Cassie would be making coffee and doing nothing else, just making the coffee. I, on the other hand, would be thinking about what I had to do, what I needed to put on the shopping list, in fact everything BUT the coffee. So, of course, my coffee would taste bitter.

Everything is energy! The food you eat has energy and the person cooking it has energy. If the cook is feeling angry or frustrated, that energy is in the food as it is being cooked and you will take that energy in as you eat it.

This hit home when I was regularly cooking dinner for a friend so she could pick it up on her way home from work. One night, she asked me what I did to her meal the night before. When I asked her what she meant, she said that she burst out laughing as she was eating it but didn't know why she was laughing.

I told her that I didn't think I had done anything different. But later, I remembered I had been thinking about a comedy show I had been watching. And so, as I was cooking the food, I was laughing at the memories.

It was a huge lesson in cooking with awareness. By giving attention to the preparation of our food, we bring awareness into its essence. If that awareness is love, then the food will taste of love.

For me, cooking is not only a mindful exercise but also a spiritual experience. It begins when I choose the people I will invite and continues when I am designing the menu, buying the ingredients, cooking, preparing the table to serving the food, enjoying the meal with my loved ones and cleaning up afterwards.

I am not thinking about my problems or world events or even about the cold weather! I am thinking about and feeling the love I have for my family and friends as well as gratitude and love to the people who grew, prepared, and brought the food to the shops.

So, if you find cooking a chore that must be done, try opening your heart and mind to a different way of cooking. If you love colour, then design your meal around the different colours.

When you are cooking, have gratitude, awareness, and appreciation for your family and friends. Offer the love in your heart to the food you are preparing for them. They will absorb it as they eat the food.

Become aware of your thoughts: when they wander, and when your mind becomes filled with your worries. Notice them, let them pass through, and then bring your mind back to the present. It may take time to cultivate this, but you can do it, of that, I am sure.

My favourite grace before eating is this one: **Thank you for the food before us, thank you for the friends beside us, and thank you for the love between us.** It is short but powerful. Try it!

Mama Rae is an extraordinary cook and universal mum whose mission is to bring love and joy into people's lives.

www.mamarae.com.au

Mama Rae's Raw Chocolate

Gluten, Dairy, & Refined Sugar Free

This is one of my absolute favourite side dishes. It tastes yummy alongside many other meals, from vegetable curries to barley loaf and roasts.

They are always a big hit with friends and family. Making them is as easy as falling off a log!

Shopping List

- ✓ ½ cup cacao butter
- ✓ ¼ cup coconut oil
- ✓ ⅓ cup coconut cream
- ✓ ¼ cup maple syrup
- ✓ 1 teaspoon vanilla
- ✓ 1 cup cacao powder

The How-To Part

1. Melt the cacao butter in a saucepan on very low heat
2. Add the coconut oil and the maple syrup
3. When melted, remove from the heat and add the vanilla
4. Add the cacao powder and mix
5. Spread the mixture thinly onto a lined tray
6. Chill for 10 minutes and cut into pieces
7. Return to the fridge to set it completely
8. Store in a covered container in the fridge
9. Enjoy!

Secrets From Mama Rae's Kitchen

- ✓ You can use, cocoa or carob powder rather than the cacao
- ✓ Replace maple syrup with your favourite sweetener
- ✓ After you have mixed your chocolate, taste it and add more sweetener if needed
- ✓ Add nuts, spices, ginger or berries for extra flavour
- ✓ Warning: don't eat this chocolate before bedtime if you are using cacao, as it is a stimulant and may keep you awake!

Wellness Tip

Cacao is high in antioxidants, magnesium, and iron.

Quick Takeaways

1

Deep breathing has an infinite number of benefits that you can access quickly and easily. Breathe in, breathe out!

2

Learning to calm your mind and body will enhance your quality of life, creativity, and your physical wellness. Calm is a superpower.

3

Find your authentic pathway to holistic parenting and raise your children from the heart.

Quick Takeaways

4

Reducing your intake of processed sugar and increasing the amount of real foods you consume can transform your physical body and state of mind.

5

The most important practice when preparing your food is to channel love and energy into the meals you make. Your body, mind and life will be touched by the love you cook with.

6

To live a life with reduced stress and increased wellness, focus on what is wholesome: your food, your mood, your loved ones, and your relationship with your body

Journal Time

It's journal time!

Use the following questions and pages to reflect inwardly on your extraordinary life.

Journalling provides us with the space to pour our feelings onto the page.

It brings us back to our truth and allows us to access the answers we need.

This alone makes it a profound practice to work with daily – and a reliable source of creativity and inspiration.

There is no judgement when you journal.

It's a record just for you – and it's there 24 hours a day. It is a sacred and safe space for you to be yourself, express what is within you, and find your way to the other side of whatever you are facing in your life today.

Use the following questions and pages to reflect inwardly on *your* extraordinary life.

Question 1

What is the next step you are going to take to create your extraordinary life?

Question 2

Which grounding practice can you embrace as part of your morning routine to clear your energy for the day ahead?

Question 3

Tune in to your inner visionary artist. Ask it for advice on what to do next. What does it say?

Question 4

Write down your intention for the next year of your life. What would you ultimately love to experience?

Question 5

Sit back and look at your home and work environment. How do you feel? What do you need to change?

Question 6

What rituals and habits can you implement to support yourself to succeed?

Question 7

What does 'living your legacy' mean to you? How can you live your legacy more powerfully?

Question 8

Write down your goals for the next three years of your life on the lines below.

Question 9

On a scale of 1-10, how committed are you to your business results? What can you do today to enhance this?

Question 10

What change can you make in your marketing to promote your business more authentically (from the heart)?

Question 11

How deeply do you breathe? Are you scared to slow down and relax? Write your thoughts on the lines below.

Question 12

What natural remedies and strategies can you use daily to calm your nervous system?

Question 13

Use the lines below to write about what holistic parenting means to you. How would you love to raise your children?

Question 14

What is your sugar intake like? Are you reliant on it? What can you do to reduce your intake of sweetened foods?

Question 15

Do you cook your food with love? What energy do you put into your food when you cook it? What energy would you love to put into it?

Your Reflections

Contact

www.extraordinarylifemagazine.com

Advertising Inquiries + Article Inquiries

Media Opportunities

Production Team

Editing: Sara Rubeck

Images Source: Shutterstock + Pexels

Typesetting: Chandrashekar Yadav

Disclaimer

The opinions expressed in *Extraordinary Life* are not necessarily those of the publisher(s). Advice is non-specific and does necessarily substitute medical, psychological or professional advice for health and wellbeing issues. We do not make any claims that anything published in this magazine is a cure for any disease, ailment or problem experienced by the reader(s). The magazine is not affiliated with any religious group or religious teaching. *Extraordinary Life* takes no responsibility for the content of advertisements. *Extraordinary Life* may alter the size, content or position of an article or advertisement where necessary. Articles, adverts, or any other part of this magazine is not to be reproduced without the prior permission of the publisher Gowor International Publishing, and all requests must be made in writing.

www.ingramcontent.com/pod-product-compliance
Ingram Content Group UK Ltd.
Pitfield, Milton Keynes, MK11 3LW, UK
UKHW060025300726
14090UKWH00019B/1077

9 780645 573435